Missing

People

VOLUME 2

Mysterious True Stories And

Gripping Missing Persons

Cases Of The Last Century:

Where Do Missing People Go?

Table of Contents

Want more books?

Would you love books delivered straight to your inbox every week?

Free?

How about non-fiction books on all kinds of subjects?

We send out e-books to our loyal subscribers every week to download and enjoy!

All you have to do is join! It's so easy!

Just visit the link at the end of this book to sign up and then wait for your books to arrive!

Introduction

I want to thank you and congratulate you for purchasing the book, "*Missing People: Mysterious True Stories And Gripping Missing Persons Cases Of The Last Century: Where Do Missing People Go?*".

Closure. People who mysteriously lost someone crave this. Whatever happened to their loved ones, whether they are still alive somewhere, or they died, the people they left behind want to know. For them, knowing the ending, no matter how horrible, is better than continuously thinking of the terrible things that they might be suffering.

In the following cases that we will discuss, closure is elusive. It's a wonder whether the families will ever find the truth behind these disappearances cases.

Thanks again for purchasing this book, I hope you enjoy it!

Chapter 1: What happened to Devin Williams?

Father of three and an attentive, loving husband, Devin Williams vanished on the fateful day of May 28, 1995. He and his family lived in Lyon County, Kansas where Devin, who was only 29 years old, worked as a long distance truck driver.

On that day, which was also the Memorial Day Weekend, Devin was delivering refrigerated goods using his ten-ton, 18 wheeler truck. His itinerary was to deliver, first to California, and then to Kansas, City. Everything was going smoothly until he reached Arizona's Tonto National Forest.

Given the occasion, many families were in the area, so imagine their shock and fear when they saw a huge truck coming their way—seemingly ready to plow into everyone.

One witness and fellow motorist, Lynn Yarington, said that Devin's truck "barreled through the trees". He even got the chance to look at the driver's face-- Lynn said that Devin had no expression, he was looking straight ahead and was not inclined to stop or slow down. He didn't even try to look if he hurt anyone. "He just kept on going," Lynn said.

When it came near the National Forest beside Kingman, Arizona, it came close to hitting several campers and their cars. Fortunately, the 18-wheeler didn't hit anything. In fact, it came to a halt in the middle of the forest where witnesses swore that they saw Devin come down from the Driver's seat, and meander around the truck.

But it was not to inspect damages, rather, they mentioned how Devin was acting bizarrely. According to them, as he roamed around his truck, it was as if he was incoherent and disoriented. He was also talking to himself. They clearly heard something about "going to jail" and "they made me do it".

Chris Hall, another camper and an eye-witness, mentioned that when Devin said something about "jail" and "made me do it", he immediately thought that people inside the truck may be in danger. Perhaps there was a hostage taking, a hijacking, or a kidnapping. But Devin didn't call for help, he didn't attempt to make the campers do anything for him.

Due to the commotion, the authorities led by Deputy Dean Wells arrived the same afternoon. He noticed that the truck was abandoned, and Devin was nowhere to be found.

As they inspected the inside of the vehicle, they noted

nothing amiss: everything appeared to be in order, so the truck was picked up by Kyle Burris of Flint Hill Transportation-- the company where Devin worked. He also accessed the National Crime Computer to see if there was a report for a missing truck or driver, but there were none.

Further investigation revealed that the route Devin trudged was his normal interstate way, but not the forest, which was 50 miles away from any highways. Looking back on his history, Devin appeared to be the good guy-- he had no known encounters with drugs and he had no crime records. His health history also revealed that he suffered no mental illness.

The inside of the vehicle, which was very clean, became a testament that nothing foul happened in the truck-- there was no violent play. The only clue to his disorientation was the call he made the day prior to his superior where he mentioned that he was having some trouble gaining sleep.

Despite this, he soundly said that he could, and he would, drive the truck. The search for Devin became a total failure-- he literally vanished without a single trace.

His wife, Mary Lou, who had last seen Devin 6 days before the fact, believed that something must have happened to her husband. For her, Devin wouldn't intentionally leave because they were "having the best times of their lives". In fact, they'd just recently bought a new house for the whole family to live in.

What could have possibly happened? Reports said that immediately after his delivery in California, Devin made a report call to Tom Wilson, who was his boss. Tom said that everything was perfect-- nothing looked troublesome. The roads he took were the normal routes and even the time frame was on the dot.

The company was even questioned due to the accounts of Devin's "incoherence" and "disorientation", but Tom insisted that he passed all the company's examinations, including the drug tests.

If the clues would be taken into consideration, whatever happened, happened on his way to Kansas, because his company said that he was okay up to the time he finished delivering the cargo in California. What did Devin mean when he said he would go to jail?

When he mentioned about "they made me do it", who were the "they" he was referring to? And what did they force Devin to do so much that he mishandled his vehicle? Where did Devin go? On foot searchers, canine patrols, and rescue teams all came up with nothing-- not even a scrap of clothing.

Well, not until two years later.

On May 2, 1997, some hikers found a skull on the Mogollon Rim-- an area which was just half a mile from where Devin was last seen. When dental exams were performed, the authorities confirmed that the skull was Devin Williams'.

Up to this point, Devin's disappearance and death are still unexplained. Due to the mystery, alien enthusiasts were in an uproar. According to Nation and World Section of The Tuscaloosa News, Devin's disappearance could be caused by Aliens. In the article entitled Vanishing Sparks More UFO Stories, Mark Shaffer said when Devin got out of the truck, he kneeled and talked to a tree.

Afterwards, he took a $20 bill and waved it in the air. He also threw rocks at the campers who tried to help him, and even threatened them that he would start a fire. Aside from his truck, he also left two things that he would never be seen without-- a police scanner and his favorite hat. Could the "they" in Devin's last words be really aliens? Enthusiasts believed so.

On a more practical and worldly explanation, netizens claim that perhaps Devin's trouble in getting sleep already persisted for days before he informed his boss about it.

Maybe the exhaustion got the better of him, so he drove the truck in a very reckless manner. When he realized what he had done, he got scared that he would go to jail. Although it didn't cover the "they made me do it" statement, many people believe it is a logical explanation.

Whatever happened to Devin could be anyone's guess now, but the mystery still persists.

Chapter 2: The case of missing Virginia Carpenter

What would it feel like if you're only child went missing-- not knowing if she was a victim of a serial killer, or she developed amnesia, and didn't know who she really was? Hazel Carpenter knew the horrible feeling when her only daughter, Mary Virginia Carpenter, disappeared mysteriously.

Then 21 year old Virginia Carpenter had brown hair and eyes. Due to appendectomy, she bore a scar on her stomach. She was also limping due to a previous bone hip infection. At the time of her disappearance, she was suffering from a severe case of sunburn. She was last seen wearing a white dress with red, green, and brown stripes.

From Texarkana, Texas, Virginia boarded a train on June 1, 1948 to return to her school dormitory in Denton, Texas. The ride lasted for 6 hours, so she had enough time to talk to a working teacher named Marjorie Webster.

Marjorie was also from Texarkana, so the two had an instant connection. When the two got off the train, they decided to call a cab to take them to their respective destinations. Marjorie was to be dropped off at the Fitzgerald Dormitories, and Virginia's destination was straight to the Texas State College For Women Dormitories.

They then hired the service of a cab driven by Edgar Ray "Jack" Zachary. When Marjorie reached the Fitzgerald dorms, Virginia remembered about her trunk luggage, which she failed to retrieve. Due to this, she asked Jack how much it would cost to drive her back to the station. Jack agreed on a price of $0.75. When that was settled, Marjorie said she could accompany her back to the station, but Virginia refused, telling her new friend that she would be alright even if she was alone.

Jack and Virginia returned to the station only to find out that the trunk would not arrive until later. The driver then suggested that he could get the luggage tomorrow and deliver it to her dormitories. Thinking that it was more practical that way, Virginia agreed.

She gave the claim receipt to the driver and signed it on the back. She also wrote down her details, which were: Virginia Carpenter, Room 200, Brackenridge. In the end, she gave Jack a dollar as an extra tip.

When they arrived at the dorm, Jack claimed that there was a yellow or a cream-colored convertible out the front. The color was not clear because it was dark--the moon wasn't shining and the streetlights were off due to repairs.

Standing by the car were two men, one was shorter and chunkier than the other.

When Virginia saw the men, she looked surprised, but not in an alarmed tone because the two men seemed to be known to her. In fact, as soon as she approached the car, the shorter of the two men lifted her up to the curb. She then instructed Jack to leave her other luggage on the ground because the boys would take it.

After fulfilling the instructions, Jack left-- leaving behind Virginia with the two unidentified men. Virginia never checked into her dorm, and she was never seen again after that.

The next day, Jack took Virginia's trunk to the front lawn, as what was instructed of him. Two days after that, it was still unclaimed so it was taken to the office. On day three of Virginia's disappearance, her boyfriend, Kenny Branham, called her mother; Hazel, because he could not reach her.

Hazel, obviously worried, called the school and learned that Virginia never checked in, and she didn't even enroll for the summer term. Hazel then called her daughter's friends and their other relatives, but they had heard nothing.

On June 5, just after midnight, Hazel filed a missing

persons report. When the police said that they would investigate the case first thing in the morning and that she should sleep first, Hazel became even more agitated, so she went to Denton to personally look for her daughter.

All avenues of searching were employed, including helicopters, motorboats, on-foot search parties, hunters and trackers. From lakes, to abandoned wells, almost all corners were inspected, but resolving the mystery was still a very hard task.

Theories of Virginia's disappearance sparked when days and days went by without any solid clue. According to her previous boyfriends, the girl was easily infatuated, so it was possible that she took off with a new love interest. Her family, especially her mother, refused to believe such a notion.

Virginia was a loving daughter, and she had great plans. In fact, she enrolled in the school for a summer term so she could pursue a science degree as a laboratory technician. Her boyfriend, Kenny, was investigated and was even subjected to a polygraph test. He passed and nothing more could link him to the case.

Jack also became a hot subject of scrutiny. According to reports, he had records of abusiveness, but aside from that, no one and nothing could connect him with

Virginia's case. His wife also stated that he was already home by 10 pm, just less than an hour after he dropped Virginia to her dorms. The time was so short that it would be hard for him to commit the perfect crime.

He also took 2 polygraph tests, and on both times, he passed. The weird thing was, in 1958, Jack's wife changed her statement. She said that Jack wasn't really home until 2:00 or 3:00 in the morning of June 2. Despite this, Jack was never charged with anything due to the lack of evidence. He became a suspect forever, up to the day of his death in the year 1987.

Some said that her disappearance could be because of the Texarkana Killings. 2 years before Virginia disappeared, 5 people were murdered, and it was suspected that the same person did it. The killer was never identified, thus, he became known as the Phantom Killer.

Of the 5 murdered people, Virginia personally knew three.

Through the course of the case, many "sightings" were reported, but none gave solid clues. One gasoline station attendant reported seeing Virginia together with two boys and another girl. She said that they were in a yellow convertible with Arkansas license plates.

After that, Mrs. James, a ticket agent in a bus station in DeQueen, Arkansas, reported seeing Virginia. She said that she saw a woman who resembled the missing lady together with a man who was 25 or 26 years old. She said that the woman appeared to be nervous, and that she asked for available hotels in the area.

When the police showed her two pictures, she pointed at Virginia's photo. However, after some time, she said that she was no longer sure if it was really Virginia. Another sighting was reported by Gladys Bass, who mentioned in a letter that they had seen a well-educated girl hitchhiking. The girl, who resembled Virginia, said that she ran away. Gladys' account, however, was not verified.

Hazel, on the other hand, believed that Virginia was a victim of amnesia. Perhaps she was alive somewhere, and she just didn't know how or where to return to. More than 6 decades later, the hope of ever finding out the truth behind her disappearance, slims down to zero.

Chapter 3: The mysterious story of Charles Horvath

A man who wanted to travel all throughout British Columbia in Canada mysteriously disappeared. Was it because he decided to hitchhike his way across the area, and then he met with a violent motorist? What really happened to 20 year old Charles Horvath?

Charles first planned to visit his father in British Columbia, but after getting the idea of travelling via free rides, he proceeded to explore the entirety of Canada by hitchhiking. It wasn't a permanent arrangement though, because he was originally from England.

The Briton told his mother (through a letter sent via fax on May 11, 1989) that they should meet in Hong Kong, to celebrate his 21st birthday and also her mother's 41st. However, before even completing the arrangement for their meeting, Charles went missing.

No matter how much she tried, Charles' mother, Denise Allan, failed to get hold of her son. So she did the next best thing which was to report him missing. On August 10, 1989, Charles' disappearance became official. Denise called the Kelowna Detachment RMCP and begged them to do something.

She also asked the local newspapers, so that she could place some ads to find her son. When none of these efforts bore fruit, she went to Kelowna together with her husband, Stuart Allan. Once she got there, she put up flyers with Charles' pictures and name. Soon after this, one woman named Joanne Zebroff, contacted them.

Joanne and her family informed Denise that they accommodated Charles in their family home. She added that when they first met Charles, it was obvious that he was a good person, but it was also apparent that he was new in Canada. He went on showing them some family photos, especially that of his mother's.

One time, Charles went to their home again, but Joanne had to refuse the visit because her brother was away. The Zebroff family ended their report by stating that they had last seen Charles in August 1989, in a night club named LiveWire.

Aside from these, Denise also learned that Charles registered at Gospel Mission. He then stayed at The Sherwoods and the Vernon Gordons family home. His last stop was in a campground in Tiny Tent Town in Kelowna. When Denise went there to inquire, the camp manager said that Charles left quickly, leaving behind the tent and all his personal belongings.

His things, like clothes, tent and sleeping bag were used by the other campers. The other items, such as the Bible and boot strap were kept. Through the efforts of the RMCP, Charles belongings were retrieved, but what worried Denise most was the fact that Charles left their family photographs behind.

She told the police that Charles never did that, that the photos were so important, that he wouldn't leave without them. Something bad must have happened that made him leave these important items behind.

At some point during the search, Denise and Stuart had to go back to England, but they also returned to Canada at a later date. When they did, they discovered a note in the hotel where they stayed. The note said *"I seen your ad in the paper, you are looking for your son. I seen him May 26. We were partying and 2 people knocked him out. But he died. His body is in the lake by the bridge."* The note was not signed, but the authorities quickly thought of the Okanagan Lake.

A lot of volunteers searched for a body, but nothing turned up. During this, a second note arrived, stating that they were searching on the wrong side of the bridge. When they started another search effort on the other side, they did find a body, but the test results confirmed that it was not Charles Horvath.

Denise didn't know what to feel. It turned out that the body belonged to a 64-year old man, and he probably died of suicide. It could be that the witness who sent the note mistook the body as Charles', but could he be right that "they were partying and two men knocked him out and killed him?"

It was at this time that a man named Gino Bourdin came up. He told Denise and the police that Charles was a good guy, and perhaps too friendly for his own good. He said that Charles often visited them at their camp to chat and to have a cup of coffee. He also reported that Charles was too trusting, that he would talk and make friends with virtually anyone. The idea was that Charles met someone with bad intentions due to his friendliness.

Or maybe, Charles planned it all along?

According to the police, they called Charles' relatives in Eastern Canada and the relatives said that Charles mentioned about wanting to disappear off the face of the planet where his mother would not find him, and then he would start a new life of his own.

Denise, however, refused to accept that. She thought that it was so out of character, that Charles loved his family, so he wouldn't abandon it intentionally. Hundreds of people claimed to have seen Charles, but no solid proof surfaced.

Denise wanted nothing more than to know what happened. If he was somewhere, maybe in a gutter, homeless and penniless, then he needed help. If he died or was murdered, he needed burying. Whatever the news, good or bad, as long as some sort of closure is given, she would gladly accept it.

Chapter 4: Tara Calico – Could a photo help this case?

In June of 1989, a shopper in a busy Florida parking lot discovered a shocking photo, facedown on the asphalt, in the space next to her car. Just moments earlier, a white van had been in its place. It appeared the driver, a mustached man in his thirties, had left the photo behind—perhaps on purpose.

In the picture, a young woman and younger boy appear to be tied up on a messy bed, their wrists behind their backs and their mouths covered with duct tape. The small space and poor lighting suggest the bed is actually a mattress inside of a van with its passenger door open, possibly the Toyota that was parked where the photo was discovered.

The young woman and boy's expressions seem afraid yet resigned, according to officials, as though they were accustomed to whatever danger they were facing. Even more alarming was that these young people looked familiar to officials: both matched descriptions for missing people, believed to have been abducted near their New Mexico homes in the previous year.

Nineteen-year-old Tara Calico, a psychiatry and psychology student at the University of New Mexico, had gone for a ride on her mother's pink mountain bike at 9:30 a.m. on September 20, 1988. Her own bike had a flat, and Tara told her mother to come looking for her if she was not home by noon, in case she popped another tire.

Tara's planned route was an impressive thirty-four total miles before lunch and a tennis appointment: It was just a workout the student actually considered to be a break. Tara worked as a bank teller on top of her full-time studies and numerous social engagements.

Her ride, however, was cut short just two miles from her house: witnesses in Valencia County reported a gray or dirty white '53 Ford truck crawling behind Tara as she rode, a few minutes before noon, along Highway 47. Tara, listening to Boston on her Walkman, appeared unaware that she was being followed.

None of the witnesses saw the actual abduction. While her mother's pink bicycle was never discovered, a piece of Tara's Walkman was found nearly twenty miles from the highway where she was last seen, near the JFK campground. Perhaps, as Tara's mother believed, the young woman threw whatever she could from the truck as clues for investigators.

The only other markers in Tara's trail were bicycle tracks

near the highway shoulder and a Boston cassette tape, discovered by her mother; police suspect this spot was where a struggle took place between Tara and her abductor.

At first, some investigators wondered if Tara's disappearance had been an accident—a hit-and-run driver, perhaps, who disposed of Tara's body to cover their trail—rather than a planned crime. The picture discovered in Florida, however, made abduction the strongest possibility, provided officials could conclusively identify Tara as the woman.

As for the young boy in the photograph, identification was not so easy. Unlike the woman—who has distinct features resembling Tara's, a unique scar on her leg that matches one Tara acquired from a car accident years before her disappearance, and a book in the photograph by V.C. Andrews, one of her favorite authors—the boy was more difficult to identify.

Initially, the theory was that he was New Mexico resident Michael Henley, a nine-year-old who'd gone missing during a hunting trip with his father in April of 1988, just a few months before Tara disappeared.

Michael's parents and Tara's mother flew to Florida to identify the people in the photo. While all were skeptical at first, they quickly identified the children as their own, even when police weren't so sure.

This photograph gave the distressed parents a great deal of hope: the type of film used to take the picture didn't exist until May of 1989, which meant the photograph was recent—and that both Tara and Michael could still be alive.

However, in 1990, the remains of Michael Henley were discovered near the site of his disappearance, and foul play was ruled out; forensics determined he'd wandered away from his father, became disoriented during a storm, and died due to elemental exposure.

It's still possible the boy in the picture was Michael, though extremely unlikely, given the location and analysis of his remains. Another possibility is that the boy in the photo is actually David Michael Borer, who went missing From Willow, Alaska, in April of 1989 and was never found.

While Tara, Michael, and David all looked very similar to those young people in the photograph, the FBI could not determine any facts or leads from the picture. While the Los Alamos National Laboratory concluded the woman in the photograph was not Tara, Scotland Yard's analysis concluded that it was.

The FBI found all results inconclusive. Another clue with flimsy promise was a sighting in southern Florida, a few days before the Polaroid was found: a group of witnesses reported a woman matching Tara's description seemingly being restrained by a group of unknown men. The lead, like so many others, gave officials and Tara's family hope, yet did not get them any closer to finding her.

Over the next few years, two more photographs, never released to the public, were discovered and identified by the Calico family as Tara: in one, a blurred face with duct tape on the mouth rests against a backdrop similar to the sheets and pillowcases in the first Polaroid.

In the second, a woman with glasses and gauze on her face—subtly binding and blindfolding her—sits next to a man authorities could not identify, on what appears to be an Amtrak train.

The photos, discovered in California, were on film not available until 1989 and 1990, respectively—although that's the only definite fact authorities were able to determine from these new photos.

Tara's mother, Patty Doel, believed with fierce conviction that all three photographs were of her daughter; Tara's sister, Michele, who didn't agree so assuredly yet does not disagree, said her mother never missed any chance to search for her daughter, aid authorities, or keep Tara's case in the spotlight.

She and her husband even went so far as to become auxiliary deputies for the sheriff's department, which allowed them to carry firearms and inform officials on the sheriff's behalf whenever they came across something that could help Tara's case.

For several years after Tara's disappearance, Patty kept her daughter's room exactly as she'd left it—even buying presents for each holiday Tara missed, and placing them on her bed. Finally, in 2003, Patty and her husband moved to Florida to begin a new life, although she never gave up hope that her daughter would be found. She brought Tara's bed and unwrapped gifts with them.

In 2011, due to failing health that was most likely exacerbated by her tireless search efforts and heartbreaking—yet never failing—hope, Patty Doel passed away. Her obituary stated that she was survived by four children, not three.

Twenty years after Tara's disappearance, a series of photocopied pictures arrived at Port St. Joe with a young boy, similar to Michael Henley, shown once as-is, and twice with black marker on his mouth to mimic duct tape. The letters were sent to the area police chief, several local churches, and *The Star* newspaper, but none contained any information about the boy, nor a return address.

They were sent from Albuquerque, thirty-five miles from Tara's home and over a hundred miles from the Zuni Mountains, where Michael's remains were found. It's been determined that the more recent photos are most likely a hoax, but police have kept them on file just in case they're legitimate or link to another case.

The same day the new photos arrived, a psychic called the sheriff of Gulf County and told him she'd had visions of Tara's body being buried somewhere in California, and that Tara's name resonated strongly in her visions.

Officials were unsure if the new photos and psychic's tip— which was not followed—arriving so close to the anniversary of the disappearance were important to the case, or if this fact only bolstered the possibility that the tips were fake.

Tara's case has received very high attention, from *A Current Affair* to *Unsolved Mysteries*, as well as *America's Most Wanted*. Oprah Winfrey also profiled her case. While police received many tips and possible sightings following each feature, and despite the efforts of many Valencia County search volunteers, no additional information could be verified.

Even the Polaroid was not a guaranteed lead; though Florida police had set up a roadblock for the white Toyota van shortly after the Polaroid was given to authorities, the van, driver, and whoever may or may not have been inside were not found.

In 2014, a woman's skeletal remains were discovered near an abandoned bunker in Valencia County. Police immediately tested the skull and torso to see if the bones matched Tara Calico's DNA, but the test was negative.

Other bones found in the area also tested negative; many were shallow-grave Native American remains, though police in the area made it clear they wouldn't stop testing. They said it's part of the search protocol, even when the search has gone on for decades.

Valencia Sheriff Rene Rivera made an announcement in 2008 that he "knew" the fate of Tara: male schoolmates, following Tara in their truck, accidentally killed her— either by striking her with the car on purpose, horsing around, flirting, or some other unknown event—and disposed of her body, then covered their crime forever with the aid of their parents.

It's not farfetched, since Tara was very beautiful and popular, but Rivera has not investigated his own claim, released any evidence, or given the boys' names—despite the fact they're men in their forties now, and no longer minors.

John Doel, Tara's stepfather, doesn't hold much hope for the Sheriff's claims. Though his wife possessed unflinching hope for Tara's return, John believes his stepdaughter died many years ago; he can't imagine this much time passing without any word or clues from Tara.

Until Tara herself, her remains, or her abductor are found, the case remains open—and officials continue to search all possible leads.

Chapter 5: Ambrose Bierce – The Civil War soldier

Few cases are as confusing as that of Ambrose Bierce, a 71-year-old Civil War soldier and writer who vanished during a trip by horse to war-torn Mexico in 1913. An enormous amount of leads—contradictory and too numerous to investigate in-depth at the time—gave Bierce a reputation as the man "who died many deaths."

The tenth of thirteen children (all given names beginning with "A"), Bierce grew up in Indiana with parents who, despite severe poverty, impressed the importance of literature upon their children.

Bierce was an avid reader and talented writer, even at a young age, although he had a strange obsession with death; he once had a dream of his own rotting, dead body, a scene he later incorporated into one of his short stories.

Bierce left home as a teenager, taking up work with a meager newspaper in his birth-state of Ohio. He enlisted in the Army Infantry a few years later, quickly becoming a lieutenant topographical engineer, responsible for mapping battlefields.

Though he was discharged from combat in 1865 following a severe head injury, Bierce continued to help with expeditions and other military matters when he could; he moved to San Francisco as a brevet major and eventually resigned from the Army altogether.

While he felt like a failure in so many aspects of his life, it's believed Bierce found solace in being a good soldier, if nothing else.

Shortly after his service in the war, Bierce married a woman named Mollie Day. Following the birth of their three children, Bierce and his wife decided to move the family to England—perhaps hoping to fuel his writing career—before moving back to San Francisco.

Later, Bierce took a job as a column and feature journalist. In 1888, Bierce and his wife divorced due to adultery on her part; Mollie died in 1889. Both of Bierce's sons died a few years later, the eldest of heartbreak-fueled suicide; the younger, of pneumonia attributed to alcoholism.

Bierce, an agnostic with severe post-war trauma and a dark sense of humor, was well-known for his *San Francisco Examiner* columns, a still-popular story called "An Occurrence at Owl Creek Ridge," and his satirical book, *The Devil's Dictionary*. His carefully-plotted horror stories continue in their popularity.

A driving force for satirical realism, many critics wonder if

Bierce's impact would be so large had he not vanished in 1913.

It's not verified why, exactly, Bierce departed for Mexico. Some theories say he was planning on interviewing revolutionary Pancho Villa for the *San Francisco Examiner*; others say he wanted to take part in the Mexican Revolutionary War, or, by contradiction, that he was racing to cover it, for reasons unknown.

Other people—undoubtedly echoing the dark and clever plots of Bierce's most beloved stories—believed his trip to Mexico and subsequent disappearance were just a way to covertly commit suicide, which Bierce publicly supported as a "noble act," or to cover up his admission to a psychiatric hospital or convalescent home.

The writer drank heavily and had endured a great deal of hardship (both on and off the battlefield) throughout his life. Prior to his trip, he made it a point to visit each site where he'd once been embroiled in battle; suicide, as well as dementia or severely failing health, were not stretches of the imagination.

Many find the entire trip to Mexico implausible, since Bierce was quite old, had not ridden a horse in many years, and suffered asthma. It's also been said that Bierce did not care for Villa's methods, military tactics, or motivation, and that it would have been unlikely he'd risk so much to join up with this army.

Another theory is that the embittered writer was losing popularity, and knew a carefully staged and oh-so-mysterious disappearance would boost his career—even if he had to remain in hiding for the rest of his life, or actually die in battle.

Regardless of his reason, Bierce was well-informed of the dangerous journey he was (allegedly) embarking upon. In a letter to a relative, he stated, "Goodbye. If you hear of my being stood up against a Mexican stone wall and shot to rags, please know that I think that is a pretty good way to depart this life." The letter is perhaps an eerie case of foreshadowing...or the first spark that would ignite a wildfire of rumors.

As World War I began, the investigation into Bierce's disappearance came to a standstill; no authorities had the time, nor the manpower, to continue the search—and with so many leads, police weren't sure where, exactly, to look.

One popular story is that Bierce was killed in the Battle of Ojinaga, the area Bierce told his secretary he'd be heading to in the last postcard he sent. Pancho Villa and his army left Chihuahua City with Bierce in tow, eager to fight.

It's said that Bierce was given a sombrero in celebration of an earlier kill, when he shot a Federale with a rifle at Tierra Blanca. Perhaps overly confident from his victory, Bierce charged prematurely at Ojinanga and got himself shot by oncoming forces.

It's nearly impossible to validate this story: if Bierce was killed in this battle, his body would have been part of a funeral pyre and burned along with hundreds of fallen soldiers, the remains long gone and unidentifiable.

The tale could hold some truth, however, as two Americans said they'd heard an elderly white man was killed in the battle, though neither could confirm if this man was Bierce.

Others claim Villa himself shot him, after Bierce apparently stole a love interest from the revolutionary and drunkenly harangued most of Villa's officers. A hot-tempered alcoholic, Bierce offending Villa to the point of murder is also not a far-fetched theory.

The story quickly transformed into another tale entirely: Bierce—now merely wounded at Ojinaga—ran from the fort just as it was invaded. A Federale, attempting to swim across the Rio Grande and reach American soil, was said to have taken Bierce with him; the old man was hurt and delirious, and the Federale figured it would be easier to enter America if he brought an American with him—

perhaps telling any officials he encountered that he simply wanted to get the man medical attention.

According to the story, the Federale and Bierce were shoved onto a refugee train. Bierce lacked clear mental capacity, as well as any form of I.D., and died without ceremony on the train, or shortly after arriving at Camp Marfa, where the train was headed.

He was buried in an unmarked grave near the camp, according to a source linked to a former Federale. Like so many others, the tale could not be verified.

Still, Bierce's death lived on: it was later reported he died near Icamole, along with a Native American, after becoming separated from Villa's army during a train raid.

General Tomas Urbina ordered their execution by firing squad, according to the story published in 1920 by James H. Wilkins, a reporter for *The Bulletin*.

Wilkins claimed he'd personally spoken with a witness in Mexico, who allegedly stole a photo of Bierce and some of his possessions from the man's lifeless body, left by Urbina to rot in the desert.

This final story seems the most plausible, given the timeline of events reported by witnesses and a corresponding account from another journalist, Tex O'Reilly, who says the owner of the house where Bierce was staying—perhaps the same man Wilkins spoke with for his article—had several items belonging to Bierce stored in the rafters of his home, including two empty envelopes addressed to Bierce.

Evidence abounding, the tales of Ambrose Bierce's fate do not stop there. Some believe the old man did not, in fact, die in Icamole, Marfa, Ojinaga, or anywhere in Mexico—that instead, he fled to Latin American after the war, a trip he'd had on his "bucket list" for many years, according to his secretary and a few colleagues.

Bierce's daughter, Helen, launched an in-depth search, but the only thing she discovered were even more stories: Bierce joined a group of spies; he died trying to get a pilfered Mayan treasure back to the States; he found a lost tribe and spent the remainder of his days in luxury, worshipped as a god among men.

Story upon story surfaced, yet none came with proof, and none led to Bierce or his body.

None of the possibilities can be verified, and as the mystery grows older, it appears nothing is there but more tall tales—now legends, not unlike the man himself. Perhaps the mystery surrounding Ambrose Bierce's death is a form of remembrance.

Whether his disappearance was an accident or staged, the

soldier-turned-writer would have liked this puzzling legacy, crafted for him by hearsay and time.

At the very least, he would have got a good laugh—his personal motto being, after all, "Nothing matters."

Chapter 6: The disappearing Sodder children

The fire that destroyed George and Jennie Sodder's home was devastating enough, but the disappearance of five of their ten children was unbearable—especially as new evidence surfaced in the rubble. It appeared the fire chief, and perhaps even the police, were planting false clues to cover their error-riddled investigation...or even their direct involvement in the children's disappearance.

It was Christmas Eve, 1945, and the Sodder family (minus son Joe, who was in the Army) were celebrating together. When George, Jennie, and their older sons called it a night, the younger children—Betty, Jennie, Louis, Martha, and Maurice, ages ranging from 6 to 14—begged for a later bedtime.

Older sister Marian had bought the children toys, and they bargained with their mother to stay up and play a little longer in exchange for chores. Jennie relented and went to bed, bringing her three-year-old daughter Sylvia with her.

A little after midnight, Jennie woke to the phone ringing. The caller, a woman, appeared to have misdialed—but when Jennie informed her of this, the woman just laughed, and the call ended.

Thinking she'd simply been the victim of a practical joke, Jennie went downstairs to check on the house. Her five children were not there; Jennie assumed they'd gone to bed, although she found it odd they'd forgotten to lock up and turn off the lights.

Jennie tended to the forgotten lights and locks, then returned to bed.

A loud noise and the sound of a rolling object across the roof woke Jennie again around 1:30 that morning, and she soon discovered the home was ablaze. She made it outside, along with her husband and four of her children; Marian carried the toddler, Sylvia.

The five remaining Sodder children were believed to still be inside the home, but all attempts to reach them proved fruitless: breaking a first-floor window, George injured himself and realized the fire now consumed the entire bottom level, making access via the stairs impossible.

When his sons tried to fetch water, they found the cold had frozen their rain barrel. George looked for his ladder, planning to climb inside and get his kids, but it was gone.

The weather also affected George's and his sons' trucks, which they'd hoped to move closer to the house so they could climb into the second story. The engines were too cold to start. George even tried to climb his home himself, but the fire was too widespread, and he wasn't able to reach the second floor.

While the Sodder men attempted rescue, Marian called the fire department from a nearby house.

Despite the fact that the Fayetteville Fire Department was barely three miles away, the firetruck didn't arrive until eight in the morning; the firemen had to be called individually, roused from sleep, and then dispatched by the operator, who hadn't been easy to reach at first, either.

By the time firemen finally pulled up to the scene, the Sodder family's home was long gone: between thirty and sixty minutes after the fire began, the home was already a pile of smoking rubble. Nothing remained.

The fire certainly seemed suspicious—its out-of-the-blue start, its rapid progression, the strange phone call Jennie had received just an hour or so prior, and the fact George's ladder was suddenly missing—yet police conducted only a brief investigation when they arrived that morning. After barely two hours, they told George the fire was caused by poor electrical wiring.

Impossible, George told them—he'd just had the wiring reinstalled, and the lights remained on for quite a while after the flames began. Regardless, police closed the investigation and dubbed it an accident.

Reports said there were no remains at the scene; the coroner's jury ruled that all five remaining Sodder children perished in the flames, and that even their bones had been destroyed, allegedly indistinguishable from the rubble of the home.

Shortly after, George removed the ashes of his home in his extreme grief, planting memorial flowers for his lost children. The fire marshal insisted that he keep the scene intact, but George continued. He didn't think his children perished in the fire, anyway—like his wife, he believed they'd been kidnapped.

Several witness reports suggested the idea wasn't just plausible, but likely: as the fire raged on, a man was seen stealing George's ladder and cutting the phone line, mistaking it for the electricity. Despite this strange behavior, the man was simply charged with theft.

He was fined, and police let him go; not once was he suspected nor questioned concerning possible involvement in the fire and disappearance of the children.

Another witness saw someone throwing "fireballs," perhaps bottles filled with accelerant and then ignited, through the windows. Police did not investigate this report much either, even when the toddler; Slyvia, found an object not unlike a napalm bomb on the property.

During the fire, a car passed by that allegedly contained the five missing children; the next morning, a waitress at a rest stop over fifty miles away said she served the kids food before they left. Their vehicle, presumably heading west, had Florida plates.

Meanwhile, another witness claimed she'd seen the children at the Charleston, South Carolina hotel where she worked. When she tried to talk to them and make conversation, the four adults they were with (two women and two men) treated her with anger and cold demeanors, then began speaking to the kids in Italian. She couldn't remember the day, and her report was not looked into very much either.

The police ruled that the fire was an accident and that the kids had, in fact, been burned inside—even when the Sodder family pleaded with them to keep the case open and follow up on the many leads and tips being received.

Jennie argued that her children's bones, at the very least, would have survived the fire: she'd recently experimented with chicken bones and flames from a stovetop, skeptical of the coroner's ruling.

When another West Virginian home was destroyed in a

fire, every skeleton of those trapped inside were uncovered; none were disintegrated in the ashes, as police insisted had happened to the Sodder kids. The police did not keep the case open, but George and Jennie refused to give up hope.

Four years after the fire, George dug up the land where his house once stood. He discovered some bones and organs, but lab tests revealed the evidence was most likely planted there—perhaps by the police and fire marshal to disguise their skimpy investigation efforts, or by the kidnappers themselves to throw officials off their trail.

According to the tests, the organ George found was beef liver, left there fairly recently; the bones were from an adolescent hand, but the likelihood of those remains surviving the fire, yet nothing else, was extremely low.

A medical expert told the Sodder family the bones were from the hand of a fourteen- to fifteen-year-old—the same age as Maurice, the oldest missing son—but George was skeptical, due to where he'd found the bones on his land.

Later testing would reveal the bones belonged to someone older, had no fire damage, and could not have been from the Sodder children. One rumor is that they came from a cemetery near the home, and were placed on the land to cover the real trail, much like the beef liver.

A couple of years after his search attempt, George and his wife invested in a billboard with their children's photographs, the mysterious story of their disappearance, and notice of a $5,000 reward (later raised to $10,000). The billboard remained up for decades, but the Sodders received no helpful tips.

Over twenty years later, George and Jennie found a photograph in their mail, allegedly of their son Louis, now in his thirties. The photo's back had this message: "Louis Sodder. I love brother Frankie. Ilil Boys. A90132". The A903132 could also be A90135, because of the confusion in the handwriting.

The photo raised suspicions: although the man in the photo could have been Louis (appearing, at least, to have Italian heritage like the Sodders), there was no proof, and the message on the back was strange.

The general consensus was that the photo was fake, a prank stirred by a recent article in the paper about the Sodder kids, but George and Jennie believed it was real— and that their children could still be alive.

They hired a private detective to try and decipher the photo's message, find the sender of the photo, or find the man in the photo. The P.I. traced a clue to Kentucky, the postmarked city for the letter, although it lacked a return address. He left, only to disappear himself shortly thereafter. He was never found.

Perhaps the most sensical and accepted theory is that the Mafia kidnapped the kids and started the fire—perhaps even bribing firefighters, police, and the fire marshal to halt the investigation—because George refused to give in to pressure from 'the mob' and shut down his coal-trucking company, or because he refused the Mafia's 'protection' or owed them money.

It's never been confirmed, but 90132—the number on the back of the picture sent to George and Jennie, supposedly of their son Louis—was the zip code for Palermo, Sicily, in the '60s. The connection could be a coincidence, but it's too significant to be dismissed.

It's been suggested that older brother Joe could have something to do with his siblings' disappearance, since he lacked an ironclad alibi that confirmed he was, in fact, away with the Army. Some also find it odd that the oldest sister, Marian, slept in the living room, yet did not notice anyone entering or leaving the house.

It's generally not believed that Joe or Marian played a part in the fire or possible kidnapping, but that perhaps they (or anyone else in the Sodder family, or related to them somehow) had enemies that would wish the family harm.

Many wonder if the man stealing George's ladder and cutting the phone line not only started the fire, but also used the ladder to take the children from their bedrooms once they'd gone to bed; perhaps a kind of smoke bomb was thrown into their rooms to knock them unconscious, or the man knocked them out by another means.

It's unlikely the older children would have gone willingly or without a fight, unless the man had accomplices to restrain the children, or a gun or some kind of weapon to threaten them into submission. It's a likely scenario, although no one was seen descending the ladder with the man.

Some suggest that the man threw each child down to his accomplices before ditching the ladder and climbing into a getaway vehicle with them, and that there was not enough light for witnesses to notice extra people or bodies.

Others wonder if the kids were somehow lured from the home, then kidnapped when they were outside; it's even been suggested that the children purposely begged their mother to stay awake longer, knowing they'd be able to slip out undetected once the rest of the family was asleep.

The reason is not known, of course, and all theories are

speculation. With a case this old and such a poorly conducted initial investigation, solid answers will only become more and more difficult to find.

George died the following year; Jennie lived another twenty years, passing away in 1989. Sylvia, just a toddler the night of the fire, continues her parents' search for answers, refusing to believe her siblings perished without a single trace.

Chapter 7: Joseph Force Crater- The Missingest Man in New York

Here's an insight into the life of a man who earned a rather unlikely title at the expense of his disappearance.

On 6th August in the year 1930, Joseph Force Crater, a Supreme Court judge of New York mysteriously disappeared on one of Manhattan's streets near the renowned and quite well populated Times Square. He was a well-groomed 41 year old chap whose disappearance made huge waves in the newsrooms and lead to launch a massive investigation which enchanted the whole country. This in turn earned Joseph Force Crater the title "the missingest man in New York."

Joseph was the eldest among the four siblings born to Irish immigrant parents – Frank Ellsworth Crater and Leila Virginia Montague. Brought up in Pennsylvania, he acquired college education at the famed Lafayette College and his law degree in the year 1916 from the Columbia University.

He began his promising career by working his way up from being a plain and inferior clerk to a fortunate and acknowledged lawyer. In doing so, he also accomplished a number of political connections in the entire city of New York over a short span of time.

In the year 1930, Franklin D Roosevelt, just a Governor back then, delegated Joseph to the state bench in April; the result was him disregarding the official candidate offered by the corrupt and powerful Tammany Hall. Post this decision and a career achievement, rumours started churning around that Crater, whose asserted fancy for the showgirls had already acquired him a disreputable and suspicious repo in his circle, had bribed Tammany bosses for his productive and well paid new job.

A few months after his promotion Joseph Crater returned to New York on 3rd August 1930 quite abruptly from a vacation in Maine. He had promised his wife Stella, who was on vacation with him, that he'd be back in a week's time at the latest, before he left. It was revealed during the investigation later, that his law clerk, Joseph Mara reported that on the morning of 6th August.

Crater demolished many documents, moved many paper portfolios to his 5th Avenue Apartment and devised for 5000 dollars to be withdrawn from his account in the bank, which was a cause for major suspicion. After leaving his office that evening, he bought a Broadway comedy ticket to the "Dancing Partner" and had a meal with his mistress, showgirl called Sally Lou Ritz, who went by the show name Ritzi, and his lawyer and friend William Klein at a Manhattan chophouse.

At first Klien, backed by Ritzi, claimed to have seen the Judge take a taxi from the sidewalk at about 9:30pm after their dinner. This claim was later changed by both as they testified saying   that they saw Crater outside the restaurant walking down the street for the last time as they entered their taxi . It was suggested by them that he was probably on his way to attend the play.

Although the judge actually disappeared on the 6th of August, it was only on September 3rd that the news of his disappearance came out! This brought about an exciting and moving manhunt along with a well-planned case analysis.

His suspicious behaviour before the disappearance lead to spawning rampant theories and guesses that he had fled with his mistress from the country or that he had probably become a victim of some putrid political play.

His startling and exaggerated story grabbed so much media attention that the phrase "pulling a Crater" became quite popular and started being used as a synonym for absenteeism all over the country, this however soon died out at the end of the investigation.

Meanwhile, comedians used the baffling and unresolved case as provisions for their stand up shows by using the line "Judge Crater, call your office" as a regular joke. Not just that, Judge Crater's name was featured in dialogues in soap operas and movies to indicate an act when something that went missing was found again or rather a mysterious body being found was connected back to being Judge Crater's.

With all of this spurning over the years of his investigation, on the request of his wife, Joseph Force Crater was declared dead legally in 1939.

In the year 2005, New York police disclosed that new clues and fresh evidence had come out in the case of the missingest man of the city. A woman who had passed away in the same year had left a handwritten note which claimed that her husband, along with many other men and a police officer had not only killed Joseph Crater, but had also buried his dead body under a section of the Coney Island boardwalk.

Back then it was a site which had been scraped and dug up during the construction of the New York Aquarium in the 1950s. It was way back when technology was not used for detecting and identifying human remains. Prior to all the evidence of the handwritten note, there was an open verdict for the case just before it was closed.

The result of this verdict was a grand jury scrutinizing this case by listening to over 95 witnesses and building up a testimony consisting of 975 pages. All the evidence in the end hit a dead-end and revealed nothing much, but claimed that he had either fallen prey to a disease like amnesia or that he had purposely disappeared or also in the gravest circumstances, was the target of a crime scene.

All in all, none of the evidence that was gathered and none of the rumours that surfaced in the bygone years proved or revealed anything related to the mysterious disappearance of the Judge Crater. We can only hope that he still lies buried under all the fishes of the New York Aquarium.

Chapter 8: Mystery behind Joseph Halpern disappearance

Joseph Halpern had a Bachelor in Computer Science in arithmetic from the University of Toronto in 1975 and a PhD in arithmetic from Harvard in 1981. In 1933, on a normal August day in Rocky Mountain National Park, Joseph Halpern, 22 years old, had put on a light blue shirt, light chestnut trousers, and substantial shoes.

He packed one orange, 4-5 sandwiches, 2 bananas and a map for the Rocky Mountain National Park motorist guide with him. He was accompanied by his parents and a college friend, Samuel Garrick. He exited his guardians at their campground, stuffed a couple of things in his backpack, and went down on a day trek with Samuel.

It was a great time for automobile tourism. By mid-evening, his companion chose to come back to the campground saying that Joseph had taken off alone to move to Taylor Peak.

Joseph stayed away forever—the stargazing graduate under study seemed to have vanished immediately and inexplicably. No trace of Joseph was found. He was an inexperienced hiker.

His nephew, Roland Halpern, had taken up the hunt began by Joseph's dad and sibling. However, in the previous 76 years, no hint of the missing explorer has ever been found.

Did he die on the mountain top? Did he get injured on the head and wander off? Did he become a victim of amnesia? Or did he just go away to start a completely new and different life altogether?

Did his college mate, Samuel know of any of his plans? Or was he the one who could have killed Joseph and buried him somewhere in the rocks? 79 years have passed since that incident and nothing can be said for sure. The mystery still remains.

"Four days of powerless anguish and no limit to it," calmed Joseph's dad Solomon to the climber's sibling Bernard, who had stayed at the family's home in Chicago. Not knowing whether Joseph was harmed, park officers and not less than 150 volunteer searchers looked over the uneven territory for quite a long time.

Four months after Joseph's vanishing, his dad came in touch with the Park's administrator. He reported his child missing to the police.

The conceivable "other reason" was the result as in passages of Joseph's letters that the family rehashed after he vanished. The young fellow said he "may turn into a homeless person" and said that the life of a cosmologist is cheerful, taking note of that "moral considerations, stresses, being, [and] loves vanish into inconsequential before this impressiveness of nature."

Bernard sent to the FBI, three of his sibling's fingerprints. The FBI chose to present them in a missing person's' record, however the organization couldn't start an examination, for Joseph's vanishing had not been disregarded any government laws.

In 1950, after proceeding with correspondence that even incorporated the private secretary of U.S. President Franklin D. Roosevelt, Joseph's guardians went to probate court and documented notification of "legitimate assumption of death."

One of the recreation centre officers who took an interest in the introductory inquiry was the late Jack C. Moo-maw, creator of "Memories of a Rocky Mountain Ranger." On Joseph, he said, "A few individuals, including the folks, are of the conclusion that the missing kid may have lost his brain and meandered away, yet I trust that, some place up there on the barrens, the wind is groaning through his bones".

Missing case of Joseph Halpern is the oldest missing person case which is entered in the NamUs System of dual databases which match the unidentified remains and the missing persons.

Chapter 9: The Marjorie hunt

The mystery of Marjorie West, a young 4 year old little girl missing since May 8, 1938 still remains unsolved. Born on June 2, 1933, no one knows her whereabouts since she was lost in White Gravel, Pennsylvania.

She has been classified as 'Endangered Missing'.

It all happened when the West family decided to take a short trip to White Gravel one morning after Sunday church service. They lived in Belford, Pennsylvania and White Gravel was only a 40 minute ride. The occasion was Mother's Day and the entire West family was enthusiastic about the road trip.

When they finally reached there, Marjorie and her elder sister Dorothea started playing in the flower valley. Around 3pm, just when Mrs West went back to the car to get lunch for the family, Marjorie and Dorothea decided to create a bouquet of violet flowers for their mother as a surprise gift for mother's day.

Just as they were finished collecting the flowers, Dorothea rushed to her mother to give her the beautiful bouquet they had created and she left Marjorie behind. When their father realized this, he scolded Dorothea for leaving her sister behind as there were high chances of rattlesnakes being hidden inside the garden.

He then ran towards the rocks to look for Marjorie. The elder brother Allan too shouted for Marjorie from behind and accompanied his father in their search.

When the West family realized their basic search had fetched no result, they finally decided to call the police. But the nearest telephone booth was 7 miles from the spot and it took some while for them to reach there. The police couldn't find anything either. In fact, the officers got worried too, they couldn't believe a little girl had vanished into thin air and they couldn't find her.

Though Mr West told the police officers about an oil field nearby and he wanted them to look there, the police completely negated it and were unperturbed. The crowd was silent with a questioned face, an anxious father, a crying mother, a worried brother, a heart broken sister and a bunch of police that didn't know what more to do.

The next day of spring came with a speculation that the girl would actually be found but who knew the fate had a never ending search involved. Civil conservation police who until the previous day were not engaged in the search as a complete unit, made it bigger the next day and expanded the search to nearby territories as well. Trained dogs from Hawthorne, New York too were left behind to find the little girl's scent.

Mayor Hugh J. Ryan, Capt. Carl L Peterson, City Engineer J. Henry Quirk, Police Chief Edward Edmunds looked in the woods along with the girl's father but produced no satisfactory result.

They expanded their search towards uplands when the 48-hour search with 21 armed men and 3 dogs produced nothing, with an assumption that the little girl might have wandered in the wooded plain. 15 square miles were traversed but with no luck again.

There had been cases of abduction near Tennessee in the early 1900s but when no one else was around, how could their daughter be kidnapped?

There was a car heading south towards Morison just before 3 and another one towards Marsh burg, right around the time when the West family arrived in White Gravel. But a grilled investigation with those car owners yielded nothing at all. The police confirmed they had nothing to do with the disappearance.

A few days later after May 8, 1933, a taxi driver from West Virginia claimed he saw a girl who resembled Marjorie's face as per description, he saw her with a mysterious man. He was in a dark coloured sedan along with the young girl.

He asked the taxi driver about the nearest hotel in the area in a hurried voice. After the taxi driver told him about an establishment right across the street, the mystery man thanked him and left the scene.

But the taxi driver saw the man again coming out with a groaned face shouting that there was not even one vacancy in that hotel and asked him if he could tell him about the nearest liquor store. The taxi driver told him that there was a bar just down the road and he could probably go there. After that, he did not come across that man again but the driver was quite sure the child with him was 4 or 5 year old.

It was few days later that he saw Marjorie's description and remembered that hurried, mysterious man. Soon, he reported the occurrence to the police. The police officer was a little confused since it is an 8 hour drive from White Gravel to West Virginia. But they didn't have any other leads so they again began the search operation.

But again, the entire hard work gave no output and the search went in vain. The man still remains unidentified.

A few days later, there was an abduction report of a young man in quite the same fashion. Also, there were reports of a woman, Georgia Tann in Memphis, Tennessee who operated an adoption agency with abducted children. She kidnapped more than 1200 young kids from 1932 to 1951.

Major areas being states bordering Tennessee and some parts of Connecticut, she helped childless couples of New York City, Los Angeles and California to adopt those abducted young little children.

All this could be related. Or maybe not...

Even after 77 years, Dorothea's granddaughter feels the sadness filled in her grandma's voice whenever she listens to the stories that took place way back in the year 1938. Though Dorothea was just 12 when this happened, she remembered every bit of it and her last words were about how much she still missed her little sister. Dorothea died in 2009.

The largest search ever made in that area tasted success only in bits but the entire truth still remains hidden. Did someone follow them from the church while they drove towards the White Gravel area? All these questions would have added to the investigation. Or maybe not.

Chapter 10: The mystery of Marvin Clark

Marvin Clark, who vanished in 1920 in the city of Oregon, is the oldest case in the database of NameUs. He disappeared in June 1920 on the way to his doctor.

A man of 63 years of age, Marvin took a stage coach to visit his doctor from his home in Oregon to his daughter's in Portland. But he never made it there.

If Marvin were alive today, he would have been 110 years of age. Needless to say, hopes of recovering Marvin alive and well have long since passed. Yet still, inexplicably, the case remained open in the hope that some new information might come to light.

For more than 50 years, there was no possible explanation as to what happened to this man who left his house in Tigard, Oregon and took a coach to Portland to visit his daughter. When his daughter reported her father missing, she commented on how he was 'well liked'.

Historians presume he was also married, due to a picture of Marvin posing with a woman who was most likely his wife. So how does a man with no enemies and a family disappear without a trace from a stage coach in his home state?

Also, the panicked daughter, Sidney McDougall, on not hearing any news about her father offered a $100 reward ($1400 in today's time) and ran an appeal in the local newspaper where he was described as well-known and well-liked. The newspaper said that he had been found and traced down to a street terminal in downtown Portland and police officers were put on for lookout for him.

But even after having so much information, Mr. Clark who had partial paralysis on his right side and couldn't use his right arm, was not found. Several days later another article was put up for him where intricate details about him were provided, such as; Mr. Clark left his home for Portland, planning on visiting his daughter, and details about his daughter Mrs. Sidney McDougall of the Hereford hotel.

The article mentioned he came to this city on bus and had been traced as far as the Yamhiti street terminal. He had gray hair, a moustache, blue eyes and was 5 feet 8 inches tall and weighed 175 pounds. He was wearing a hat and a dark suit. Mrs. McDougall had offered a $100 reward on any information leading to the locations of her father.

The case went cold until May 10 1986. A body was discovered by Loggers who were clearing an isolated section of Portland when they discovered remains of a mystery man who must have been there for at least half a century.

This body was found next to a very old revolver, along with some other age appropriate items such as an 1888 nickel, a pocket watch, a 1919 penny, leather shoes, wire-rimmed glasses, a fraternal order of eagles pocket knife and four tokens. A historian later told that the tokens could have been tavern tokens won in card games and likely to be used to buy food or drinks.

Police also found a corroded revolver around the body and an expended .32 caliber bullet. A single shot had entered the skull at the temple. Clark's daughter came forward saying that it might be her long missing father. But the case was far from closed.

The body had degraded to such an extent that there was no way of identifying it. The unidentifiable body was declared a suicide by the coroners and that was that, as they say, at least for another 20 years.

After a certain amount of time, the assumption in the case was taken as truth so that the resources of the police were not wasted for nothing. On top of this, a case simply can't remain open when there are no leads to go on and no possible way of identifying the body or resolving the issue.

But this wasn't convincing enough for Dr. Nici Vance from the Oregon state medical examiner's office, whose interest in the case was sparked last year. Vance was determined to solve one of America's oldest missing person cases. With advancements in technology and DNA testing, Vance was able to make a tenuous DNA connection between Clark's body and his great-great-grandchildren from the paternal line.

This evidence wasn't enough to be conclusive until Vance found a relative of Clark's from the maternal line to close the case. And that was the end. Case closed. Vance concluded absolutely that the body found in 1986 was Marvin Clark's who had died by suicide and America's second oldest missing person case and was closed in 2014.

But for many people, this case still remains a big mystery. Why did Marvin Clark kill himself?

Clark seemed happy and had a family. That is not to say that people can't suffer from depression or have problems and still seem happy on the surface. My question is this:

why would Marvin Clark arrange to see his daughter on the day that he died?

If he was unhappy, why wouldn't he take himself somewhere quiet and do the deed? Again, all of this is only speculation. We will never know the situation or what was going through this man's head on the day that he died. What the DNA tests still haven't managed to explain however is why the body of Marvin Clark was assessed to be between 30 and 50 when he died by coroners whereas his daughter informed the press that Clark was in his seventies when he died.

So what could have happened to him? Well there are many possible theories that go around in this case. Such as; he used the visit to his daughter as an excuse and maybe he was in failing health and may have had enough and had decided to end his life. But one question remains as to why he would do such a thing while visiting his daughter?

Maybe as an escape plan to officially declare himself dead and to live whatever amount of time he had left, in solitude. Well we just hope they solve the mystery case, his next of kin could claim his belongings and most importantly give the man a proper burial and then his soul may rest in peace finally.

Chapter 11: Jean Spangler- the unsolved mystery

Jean Spangler was an American dancer, part-time actress and a model. She used to live with her 5 year old daughter Christine, her mother Florence, sister-in-law, Sophie and her brother Edward in LA, California. In the year 1942, she got married to Dexter Benner, a manufacturer but got divorced later in the year 1946.

Jean had been trying to set her foot strong in Hollywood. Even though a small time actress, she was strikingly beautiful and had the desire to make it big. She was well known in the circuits of Los Angeles for her glamour and grace.

It was on October 7th, 1949 at 5pm on that fateful day, she left her house in Wilshire Boulevard LA. She had talked to her sister in law, Sophie before she left, and asked her to watch over Christine (her daughter) while she went to meet her ex-husband and discuss about child support payment.

But she never returned.

She was last seen by a clerk of a local store, he remembered seeing her on that day and she appeared to be waiting for someone. She was never seen again by anyone after that. Police registered a missing case the next day.

Investigation and hunting for Miss Jean started with full swing. Police tried to put together the possibilities and examined involvement of her ex-husband, Dexter Benner, but to no avail. As per Dexter, she never visited him that day. Not just that, she had not even talked to him in the past several weeks.

Dexter Benner's new wife, to whom he had been married for a month, confirmed that Benner was with her at the time of the disappearance. She did not leave the house that day to meet Dexter at all. So, where did she go? The hunt was on.

"Glamour Girl's Body Hunted" was making the headlines in the newspapers. Two days later, her purse was found near Fern Dell entrance. The straps were torn on one side of it which made it look as if someone has snatched it off from her. There was no money in it.

It was not an unusual thing, since Jean hadn't carried any money that day. That turned down the possibility of a robbery. Approximately 60 police officers and over a hundred volunteers searched the 16.62 sq. km natural terrain park but no further clues were unearthed. However, what made the investigation complex and the case all the more mysterious was the note found inside the purse.

The note was addressed to 'Kirk'. The words that were found in Jean Spangler's note just 2 days before her mysterious disappearance said that she could not wait any longer and was going to see Dr. Scott. The note ended with a comma. It seemed like she wrote it in a hurry and stopped midway.

It talked about Dr.Scott. No man with these names existed in Jean's life. Investigations lead to several directions; according to her mother, Jean was meeting someone named Kirk and he had even picked Jean up from her house couple of times, but remained in his car every time.

Actor Kirk Douglas, who also starred in the movie "Young Man with a Horn", was vacationing in Palm Springs at the time of the disappearance. When questioned by the head of the investigating team, he denied knowing Jean as a person.

Robert Cummings, the star of Pretty Girl, had been working on trying to throw some light on which the "someone" might have been. He recalled a conversation he had with Spangler in which she had mentioned she had a new romance in her life. Though it wasn't serious, but she seemed ecstatic. Kirk, whom Jean was referring to, was never to be found.

On the other side, some of Jean's friends claimed that Jean was three months pregnant at the time of her disappearance. This boosted the chances of a possibility that she was planning to visit a doctor to get the baby aborted which was illegal at that time.

Police looked for a clue and met all doctors with the last name Scott around LA but Jean had never visited any of them. Police also looked for a medical student, infamously known as "doc" who helped with abortions. All efforts lead to no substantial breakthrough.

Another theory said Jean would have eloped with Davy Ogul. Davy was the assistant of mobster Mickey Cohen, and had disappeared exactly two days after Jean. It was believed that Spangler and Ogul disappeared wilfully to avoid prosecution for conspiracy. This remained a possibility but could not be proved.

Spangler's case got nationwide media attention. A generous reward of $1000 promised by columnist Louella Parsons for information regarding Spangler's disappearance or her location also didn't turn up anything. The case remains a mystery.

There were rumours of sightings of Spangler in Northern and Southern California, Mexico City, Phoenix and Arizona over the next two years of her disappearance but none of them were validated.

Many people have claimed to have spotted Spangler since her disappearance in 1949, although none of them could be verified. In 1950, a customs agent claimed to have seen Ogul and Spangler together in an El Paso hotel. Even the hotel clerk identified a photograph of Spangler and confirmed that a lady looking very similar to the picture was at the hotel.

However, the hotel register never had names of either Ogul, or Spangler.

Many theories were put forward: Spangler was killed by the mysterious "Kirk" when she tried to blackmail him. She was killed in a mob hit on Davy Ogul and now shares her grave with him and Frank Niccoli in the desert near Palm Springs. Spangler was killed by her ex-husband. Spangler's old lover "Scotty" returned and killed her in a fit of rage and jealousy...

But none of the theories could answer the questions: Was

she avoiding being detected? Was it really Spangler who was in that hotel? Who was Kirk? Whom did Spangler meet on that fateful day of October 7th? Where is Ms. Spangler? What happened that she had to leave her daughter Christine for whom she fought a custody battle for for two years? This case still remains open with LAPD, and Spangler is still missing.

Chapter 12: **Natalee Holloway-disappeared leaving no clue behind**

Natalee was a good looking 18 year old girl from the rich outskirts of Mountain Brook, Alabama. She was a bright student and was part of the National Honour Society. She participated in extracurricular activities and also, was part of her school's dance team.

On May 26th, 2005, Natalee travelled to Aruba along with 124 other batch-mates. They had just graduated from high school. They were scheduled to travel back to Alabama on May 30th, exactly 4 days later.

Natalee never made it to the airport on the 30th.

Later, her packed luggage and passport was found in her hotel room. However, Natalie was nowhere to be seen. The missing case of Natalee Holloway is one of the most unfortunate incidents which can never be erased from memory of this generation.

Her disappearance created such a nationwide sensation for over half a decade that the media frenzy was criticized for the extent of coverage. 10 years since that day, a lot of water has flown across the river.

Her parents, Jug and Beth Twitty landed the same day in Aruba. According to her schoolmates, Natalee was last seen with three young fellows, at 1:30 AM, at a local nightclub. The three males were 17 year old Joran van der Sloot, 21-year-old Deepak Kalpoe and his brother, 18-year-old Satish Kalpoe.

There were many versions of what happened on that fateful day. Many have been arrested, released and rearrested over the years. These names remain as suspects even to this date.

Holloway's parents were pressing for enquiry against the three males right from the day they landed in Aruba. Van Der Sloot's statements which followed were no less than playing a cruel game with Holloway's parents. According to sources, he denied knowing Holloway in the beginning.

Later he confessed that Holloway was with them on the night of the 30th and they drove along California Lighthouse, only to come back to the hotel and drop her back at 2AM. Van Der Sloot also informed them about two well-built black coloured men approaching Holloway as they drove away after dropping her.

People of both nations came together in a rare show of compassion and searched for Holloway for the next month. Hundreds of Americans, Arubans, and even Dutch marines looked for Holloway along the beaches and oceans. The Aruban government declared holiday for its officials and civil servants to help in the search. Aruban government collected and donated 20,000 USD for aid of search volunteers. All to no avail.

Police investigation was moving swift on the other side. There was heavy involvement of US investigative agencies right from the beginning. The first arrest related to the case was of two former security guards of a nearby hotel.

They were released without pressing any charges within days. On June 9th, Van der Sloot, along with the Kalpoe brothers were arrested. In between, a DJ named Gregory Croes, Paulus Van der Sloot, father of Joran Van der Sloot, were also arrested. There were so many clues that the case was about to see a breakthrough very soon. Meanwhile, the stories from Van der Sloot and his friends kept changing.

This time they said that Van der Sloot and Holloway were dropped at a beach near Marriott hotel by the Kalpoe brothers. Van der Sloot claimed that he left Holloway there alone and walked back to his house. There were many leads and eyewitnesses who claimed that they had seen Van der Sloot on the 30th in the early morning hours.

Landfills were searched; a lake was dried, all in search of Holloway. Everything turned fruitless.

Meanwhile, police rearrested the Kalpoe brothers and a separate case of criminal activity was filed against them related to an incident of sexual abuse of an under aged girl. It was widely accused as an act of pressuring the three suspects. The court released all three on September 3rd and removed all restrictions on them within the next ten days. Van der Sloot was let go free.

It was almost a year since her disappearance by April 2006. There were more arrests and releases in 2006 related to the case. Geoffrey Cromvoirt, a drug dealer and son of a Dutch politician were arrested but released soon. Meanwhile, Van der Sloot was giving interviews for news channels and writing books about his knowledge of the Holloway case.

In 2007 all three were arrested and released for a third time. This time the court was vocal and suspended the case lacking any evidence to prove violent death of Holloway. However, the story was not over yet.

In February 2008, the Dutch media broadcasted a video in which Van der Sloot had openly admitted to have committed murder of Miss Holloway. The video was shot by a journalist named Peter Vries.

This was a sensation and police announced the reopening of the case within hours of the news going public. As expected Van der Sloot denied any involvement and said that the recording was made while was under the influence of Marijuana.

Peter Vries himself later got into trouble after a secret video of him admitting to false motive behind the Van der Sloot interview. The court later decided that the interview could not be considered as a confession and Van der Sloot was off the hook again. In November of the same year, Van der Sloot went on to tell that Holloway was sold to a sexual slavery gang and shipped off to Venezuela during a Fox News interview.

Van der Sloot's whims didn't stop there. In March 2010, Van der Sloot contacted Beth Twitty's attorney and asked for money in exchange of information related to the death of Natalee Holloway. The family did pay him 25000 USD, and in exchange, Van der Sloot created yet another imaginative story as always.

History repeated again, probably this time to put an end to it. On May 30th of 2010, exactly 5 years after the disappearance of Natalee Holloway, a Peruvian student

Stephany Tatiana Flores Ramírez went missing.

She was found dead three days later in a hotel room which was hired in the name of none other than Van der Sloot. He was arrested in Chile and deported to Peru. He admitted to killing both Ramirez and Natalee while in custody in Peru.

On January 11th, 2012, Van der Sloot was sentenced to 28 years of Jail term. On January 12th, 2012, a judge in an Alabama court passed an order calling Natalee Holloway as officially dead. The frenzy about the missing case of Natalee Holloway rested after this. However, even today nobody knows where Natalee rests.#

Conclusion

Thank you again for purchasing this book!

Unexplained disappearances are something not to be taken lightly. Just imagine, how could someone not be found when in almost all corners, authorities and concerned, vigilant people are on the lookout?

If they were murdered, then why does the perpetrator have the ability to hide the body without a law enforcers' knowledge? If they willingly disappeared, how come no solid tip was observed? Perhaps their disappearances are ought to teach us a lesson, that anything can happen to anyone.

If you enjoyed this book, do you think you could leave me a review on Amazon? Just search for this title and my name on Amazon to find it. Thank you so much, it is very much appreciated!

Check Out My Other Books

Below you'll find some of my other popular books that are popular on Amazon and Kindle as well. You can visit my author page on Amazon to see other work done by me. (Seth Balfour).

True Ghost Stories

UFOs And Aliens

Conspiracy Theories

Missing People

Serial Killers

Cannibal Killers

Missing People – Volume 2

You can simply search for these titles on the Amazon website with my name to find them.

Want more books?

Would you love books delivered straight to your inbox every week?

Free?

How about non-fiction books on all kinds of subjects?

We send out e-books to our loyal subscribers every week to download and enjoy!

All you have to do is join! It's so easy!

Just visit the link below to sign up and then wait for your books to arrive!

www.LibraryBugs.com

Enjoy :)

Made in the USA
Las Vegas, NV
09 March 2022

45304291R00051